Guest Book

(Name and Email Edition)

By

Matthew Harper

www.matthewharper.info

Guests

Names	Email Address

Thank You:

Guests

Names	Email Address

Thank You:

Guests

Names	Email Address

Thank You:

Guests

Names	Email Address

Thank You:

Guests

Names	Email Address

Thank You:

Guests

Names   Email Address

Names	Email Address

Thank You:

Guests

Names   Email Address

Thank You:

Guests

Names	Email Address

Thank You:

Guests

Names	Email Address

Thank You:

Guests

Names	Email Address

Thank You:

Guests

Names	*Email Address*

Thank You:

Guests

Names   Email Address

Thank You:

Guests

Names	Email Address

Thank You:

Guests

Names   Email Address

Names	Email Address

Thank You:

Guests

Names   Email Address

Thank You:

Guests

Names   Email Address

Thank You:

Guests

Names   **Email Address**

Thank You:

Guests

Names	Email Address

Thank You:

Guests

Names	Email Address

Thank You:

Guests

Names   Email Address

Thank You:

Guests

Names   *Email Address*

Thank You:

Guests

Names

Email Address

Thank You:

Guests

Names	Email Address

Thank You:

Guests

Names   Email Address

Thank You:

Guests

Names   Email Address

Thank You:

Guests

Names	Email Address

Thank You:

Guests

Names   Email Address

Thank You:

Guests

Names	Email Address

Thank You:

Guests

Names   Email Address

Thank You:

Guests

Names   Email Address

Thank You:

Guests

Names   Email Address

Thank You:

Guests

Names

Email Address

Thank You:

Guests

Names   **Email Address**

Thank You:

Guests

Names	Email Address

Thank You:

Guests

Names	Email Address

Thank You:

Guests

Names   Email Address

Thank You:

Guests

Names	*Email Address*

Thank You:

Guests

Names	Email Address

Thank You:

Guests

Names   Email Address

Thank You:

Guests

Names   Email Address

Thank You:

Guests

Names   Email Address

Thank You:

Guests

Names   Email Address

Thank You:

Guests

Names	Email Address

Thank You:

Guests

Names   Email Address

Names	Email Address

Thank You:

Guests

Names	Email Address

Thank You:

Guests

Names

Email Address

Thank You:

Guests

Names

Email Address

Thank You:

Guests

Names	Email Address

Thank You:

Guests

Names	Email Address

Thank You:

Guests

Names   Email Address

Thank You:

Guests

Names   *Email Address*

Thank You:

Guests

Names   *Email Address*

Thank You:

Guests

Names	*Email Address*

Thank You:

Guests

Names	Email Address

Thank You:

Guests

Names	Email Address

Thank You:

Guests

Names	Email Address

Thank You:

Guests

Names   Email Address

Thank You:

Guests

Names   Email Address

Thank You:

Guests

Names	Email Address

Thank You:

Guests

Names   Email Address

Thank You:

Guests

Names	Email Address

Thank You:

Guests

Names   Email Address

Thank You:

Guests

Names	Email Address

Thank You:

Guests

Names	Email Address

Thank You:

Guests

Names	Email Address

Thank You:

Guests

Names   *Email Address*

Names	Email Address

Thank You:

Guests

Names	Email Address

Thank You:

Guests

Names | Email Address

Thank You:

Guests

Names   Email Address

Thank You:

Guests

Names   *Email Address*

Thank You:

Guests

Names   *Email Address*

Thank You:

Guests

Names   Email Address

Thank You:

Guests

Names	Email Address

Thank You:

Guests

Names

Email Address

Thank You:

Guests

Names	Email Address

Thank You:

Guests

Names   Email Address

Thank You:

Guests

Names   Email Address

Names	Email Address

Thank You:

Guests

Names	Email Address

Thank You:

Guests

Names	Email Address

Thank You:

Guests

Names   Email Address

Thank You:

Guests

Names	Email Address

Thank You:

Guests

Names	Email Address

Thank You:

Guests

Names   Email Address

Thank You:

Guests

Names   Email Address

Thank You:

Guests

Names   Email Address

Thank You:

Guests

Names   Email Address

Thank You:

Guests

Names   Email Address

Thank You:

Guests

Names	Email Address

Thank You:

Guests

Names	Email Address

Thank You:

Guests

Names   ### Email Address

Thank You:

Guests

Names	Email Address

Thank You:

Guests

Names   Email Address

Thank You:

Guests

Names   Email Address

Thank You:

Guests

Names   **Email Address**

Thank You:

Guests

Names   **Email Address**

Thank You:

Guests

Names   Email Address

Thank You:

Guests

Names   Email Address

Thank You:

Guests

Names	Email Address

Thank You:

Guests

Names   Email Address

Thank You:

Guests

Names   Email Address

Thank You:

Guests

Names   *Email Address*

Thank You:

Guests

Names	Email Address

Thank You:

Guests

Names	Email Address

Thank You:

Guests

Names   Email Address

Names	Email Address

Thank You:

Made in the USA
Middletown, DE
13 September 2023

38450417R00060